THE TASK FORCE THAT SAVED CHRISTMAS

JACK GANNON

CYNDI WILLIAMS-BARNIER

JACK GANNON & CYNDI WILLIAMS-BARNIER

ISBN-13   978-1-7339992-3-6
ISBN-10   1-7339992-3-6

Editing by Bill Barnier
Cover design and Interior formatting by Jack Gannon

AUTHORS' NOTE

These stories take place in chronological order between "Murder In Twos and Threes" and "Trail of The Talon", also by the authors.

BY THE AUTHORS

TASK FORCE SERIES in chronological order

Murder In Twos and Threes
Trail of The Talon
Trail of The Hunter
The Latrodectus Murders

THE INSPECTOR SERIES

Dawn of The Living Ghost
Tears of Destiny

STAND ALONE

Tales On The Yellow Brick Road

I Walked In Santa's Boots: Lowcountry Christmas
Memories (by Jack Gannon)

SILENT NIGHT, MURDER NIGHT

Billy Lawrence locked the front door of his dry-cleaning shop and flipped the switch that lowered the security bars outside the glass front entrance. His assistant, Frederica Adams, locked the back door after verifying their police escort had arrived behind their store in the strip-mall.

"Had a good day," Fred remarked, returning to the register to print out the daily receipt report.

"Yeah," Billy said quietly. "Always do before Christmas. People want their suits pressed and dresses cleaned for Christmas Masses and parties and such."

Fred looked at Billy, studying him. "You never seem excited about it."

Billy looked at the young strawberry-blonde woman and smiled. "Ah, Frederica," said the 50-year-old black store owner, "I love Christmastime, but I celebrate it here." He tapped his heart gently. Billy's black eyes glistened when he spoke; actually, they glistened most of the time. Fred knew it was exactly as he'd said – happy all the way through to the heart.

"That's beautiful," she replied. "You know you're welcome to join us for Christmas dinner. My daughter always loves to see her 'Uncle Billy', especially when there's food involved."

Billy continued to smile. Fred's daughter, Anna, was a little blonde body of bubbly energy, and she never failed to make Billy grin. Fred knew Anna was the only one who made him smile joyously, as opposed to the friendly, warm courtesy smiles he gave their customers. Raising an eyebrow, he replied, "You tell my little 'niece' I send my love." He spoke slowly, his tired voice gravelly.

"You're such a spiritual man," Fred said, not for the first time. "You could almost be a priest, the way you sound sometimes."

"Not my callin'," he replied. "I'm happy to be right here." He took the register till to the office, Fred following behind. He put the till on her desk to prepare the bank deposit, then sat at his own desk to do his store's end-of-day paperwork.

"Well," said Fred as she counted cash, "do you have any plans for Christmas?" She looked up at his light brown face, slightly wrinkled, and stared at the dusting of freckles on his nose.

"Nope," he replied, unceremoniously. "Just the same as always. A quiet dinner, watch 'It's A Wonderful Life', and have a peaceful night of personal reflection—with my poodle, Mixie, of course." He got a sudden image of his white poodle nestled by his side on the couch, begging for bits of left-over turkey from his plate. He chuckled aloud at the thought.

Fred clicked her tongue and shook her head. "Doesn't sound very Christmasy to me." She'd tried for five years, ever since he hired her, to coax him to join her and her husband for Christmas dinner, especially after Anna was born. When Fred's husband was murdered in Iraq by terrorists, Anna immediately shut down and refused to talk to anyone. She became despondent, and barely ate. Fred once brought Anna into work with her one day, when the little girl was sick…

She hadn't had time to ask Billy ahead of time, but hoped he'd not object. However, he warmly welcomed the little, sickly Anna with a kind hug, and set her up in the office. Billy then stepped out of the store for a few minutes, hurrying down to a few of the mall stores, and came back with several toys for the five-year-old to play with while he and her mommy worked. When he walked into the office, Anna woke from her feverish sleep on the office couch, and rubbed her eyes. Though she was ill, the little girl looked up at the tall man and smiled. Fred watched from the doorway, eyes tearing from the kind bonding moment taking place in front of her. She was overjoyed from the first complete act of pure kindness she'd ever witnessed.

"A place is always set for you, you know."

"It's greatly appreciated, thank you."

She finished her cash counting and started reconciling the credit card payments. "Well, it's still a week away. You never know when a Christmas miracle might happen," she teased him.

Billy replied, "Yes, a Christmas miracle..."

Fred locked the deposit bag and placed it in her purse to take to the night deposit with her regular police escort. She put on her heavy denim coat as Billy slipped into his worn brown leather jacket atop a green V-neck sweater, and pulled on a matching woolskin cap.

She was about to wrap her red scarf around her neck, but decided against it and left it hanging on the coat rack. They walked down the hall and stopped at the back entrance. "You know," she said, "I've never told you how much I appreciate you being closed on Sunday. It's nice to have a day off with my baby...and I've started going back to church. Did I tell you?"

Billy smiled. "No, you didn't! I'm very proud of you."

"It's nice, you know? And Anna is so good during the services. Not a word, unless it's during the prayers and all." She buttoned up to prepare for the cold air outside. "You're welcome to join us sometime for service, you know."

"Perhaps one day."

She turned to activate the alarm as he looked out the backdoor peephole.

The police officer was slumped over the steering wheel, his arm hanging out the window. A familiar face was standing within feet of the back door of the dry cleaners, and another man was in the distance, walking away from the patrol car.

"Fred!" he yelled. He grabbed her by the arm and practically dragged her away from the back door. "Run!"

They were only steps down the hall when the back door exploded inward...

Billy's eyes opened slowly. He was sitting, yet

slumped forward, his vision blurred. He finally realized he was looking at the floor, sheetrock rubble, fragments of the door, and his hat covered in dust. He had the unmistakable iron-like taste of blood in his mouth.

He shook the cobwebs from his brain and raised his head gently, trying to take stock of his position. He finally realized he was tied to his desk chair, his hands bound behind the chair back. Beside him sat the still-unconscious Fred, her head down and a small line of blood dripping off her nose to the floor. Billy pulled at his bonds, realizing there was no way to escape.

"'Bout time you woke up, Papa," said a long-lost voice behind him.

Billy rotated his desk chair toward the source of the voice. His eyes widened in recognition of the man's face.

A stout black man stood with his hands crossed in front of him. He wore a snug, dark blue Armani suit—the jacket fit so tight it seemed the front two buttons would burst off. Large, gold-jeweled rings adorned each pinky finger. Beside him stood a much shorter Asian man, the one Billy saw outside the door before it exploded inward. Armani Suit spoke in a deep, baritone voice, "You been very hard to find, Papa. But I found you. You finally gonna pay your debt to me..."

Outside, a second police cruiser slowly drove down the back alleyway of the mall. The lights from his car clearly illuminated the first police car, and the arm hanging out the window. "Central," said Corporal Carter into his microphone. He put the car in park further back from the first car and used the car's spotlight to check the building doors and windows. He saw the door had been crashed in and the officer in the car was apparently unconscious or dead. "Central, send backup to my location, behind Lawrence Dry

Cleaners—officer down, probably B&E, send backup units and medical, and put SWAT on standby."

"10-4, Corporal," said the female voice coming from his police radio.

Carter got out of his car, Glock drawn, leaving the engine running and the car door locked, per protocol. The lithe detective gradually advanced on the other cruiser, wary of every sight and sound as he neared the squad car. He reached the front passenger door and peered in. The window had been smashed inward—the bullet's exit wound in the officer's head gave confirmation that he was obviously dead. He moved a foot toward the front of the cruiser, staring at the remains of the door of the dry cleaner. An explosion of red was the last thing he saw before blackness engulfed him.

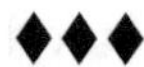

Another Asian man entered Billy's office and whispered in Armani Suit's ear. The black man said, "Well, Papa, looks like we're gonna be adding some more friends to our little party." He looked at the slowly-stirring Fred. "You wanna tell your girlfriend here who you really are? Or shall I?"

Colonel Tom Mickelson, United States Marine Corps, Retired, and director of the secret federal Task Force Division, looked up when his assistant opened the door without knocking. A tall blond man in a gray suit, black tie, and patent leather shoes entered without a word. Tom's assistant closed the door behind him and returned to his own office. Tom removed his bifocals, placing them on his desk, and eased back in his squeaky leather chair. "Well, Vance," said Tom dryly, "you still make your grand entrances."

"Witty as ever," said Vance, taking a seat across from the director. "Tom, we have a situation." He handed Tom a manila folder.

Tom read its contents. "How did they find him?"

"We're still working on that," said Vance. "While we figure out the how, we need to take care of the now."

Tom keyed in a command on his desktop computer and eyed the result quickly. "Agent Seeker was the original one who brought in our witness, but he's unavailable."

"Which one of your agents *is* available?" Vance asked, more demanding than inquiring.

Tom gave a sly grin when he saw which of the four Task Force field agents was currently not on assignment. "Spy is currently between assignments."

He looked up and saw Vance barely smile. The stoic man rose and asked, "How close is he?"

"He's actually here in D.C. He's supposed to be heading back to Richmond within the hour."

"How fast can he get to Centreville?"

"He'll come right past us on the way..."

Mark Jason, president of Jason Enterprises and the leader of the Task Force field team, walked hurriedly into Tom's office minutes later. "What's the emergency?" asked the muscular, bearded executive.

Tom rose. "Walk with me to your staging area." The two men left the office and walked down the hall to the team's main preparation area for major assignments. "Several years ago, there was a man who was an employee for a New York 'family', although he didn't know it. He was a gentle man who worked as a guidance counselor for a neighborhood boys and girls center."

Mark and Tom stopped at a metal, double-pocket door with no doorknobs, only an optical reader beside the doors. Mark looked in it and a gentle green light shone briefly into his eyes.

"Verified, Spy," said a female voice, and the double doors receded into either wall. They walked into a dark room that immediately flared to brightness when they entered.

There were four closed doors leading to matching wardrobe areas. Each door had a different geometric symbol: a triangle, a circle-in-a-circle, two upside-down triangles, and a diamond. They walked to the diamond symbol, upon which Mark placed his right palm. The wardrobe doors opened, revealing several black uniforms, sets of boots, and gloves. A second door opened to reveal black gun belts, each with a flat metal buckle with the same diamond symbol. "So, what about this counsellor?"

"It was the old story: being in the wrong place at the wrong time."

"Do tell," Mark said as he removed his clothing.

Tom took a seat while Mark hung up his suit and began to pull on one of the black, bullet-resistant, partially computerized one-piece uniforms. He struggled slightly while putting it on.

Tom's eyebrows crinkled at the site. "Picked up some weight there, Mark?"

"Ah, no. Actually, well—um, Jan's been extra helpful with some, um, muscle toning lately. Bought a foreign book…"

"Yeah, yeah I know all about the Kama Sutra. Just schedule time for re-measurements and requisition a bigger suit; you're embarrassing me with your grunts and groans."

"Um, yes, sir, soon as I'm done, sir," he replied, smiling. He zipped up the front of the suit and sealed the material with a wave of his hand over the biometric circuitry in the fabric. "Go on."

"He kept a perfect schedule at his neighborhood youth activity center, and the 'family' regularly used the center after hours for some of its more illicit meetings. One particular meeting was also a trap; a planned assassination of a rival 'family' patriarch. Unfortunately, that one particular night our witness left his cell phone, of all things, on his desk, and went back for it. He entered the center right at the second the rival patriarch was killed on the gym floor with a single shot to the head. Well, our guy high-tailed it outta there and right to a phone to call the cops. So, he immediately went into police protection, testified about the murder, never realizing until after the trial that he saw his own 'family' boss doing the killing."

Mark adjusted the knee-high leather boots and inserted several small weapons and items in hidden pockets within, then did the same to the elbow-high leather gloves. "So he ended up with an entire 'family' wanting his head on a silver platter?"

"Yup," said Tom.

He watched Mark pull the solid black hood over his head and seal the seam to his uniform top. The biometric material locked together, and only Mark's physiological fingerprint, or one of the other agents, could undo the connected fabric. He grabbed one of the black leather holsters and locked it around his waist. Mark opened a gun cabinet and withdrew a black-plated .45 automatic, which he placed on the metal slat with extended clips that hung from the holster over his right hip. He held the gun in place, while the clips' sensors read his biological signature and locked the weapon to the slat. Finally, he grabbed several black leather pouches which he attached around the circumference of his belt; each one contained a new bullet magazine.

"He was set up under witness protection as a dry cleaner shop owner in Centreville. He's done everything exactly as prescribed under witness protection, but about an hour ago he was found by the 'family' and he and his employee have been intercepted in his shop."

Mark looked at him through the horizontal ebony black tear-drop shaped lenses in his hood. "'Intercepted'? You don't know if he's alive or dead?"

Tom looked at him sternly. "That's your job to find out. And if he is still alive..."

Mark tapped the vocoder in the hood below the larynx, turning his regular baritone into an electronically-enhanced bass. "Understood."

Mark closed his wardrobe doors and drawers, which automatically locked shut. Rapidly he walked down the hall toward the Division garage complex. The door opened at his approach and he stepped through without slowing. There were four bay doors, and a black sports car was parked in front of one. Spy approached the driver's door and it unlocked automatically as the passive sensors recognized its assigned driver. The agent slid into the driver's seat and the door closed on its own. He pressed the ignition button on the steering column; the engine roared to life. The bay door immediately opened and the agent guided the car backwards out of the bay, turned around, and gunned the car's engine to rocket the car toward the Division grounds' exit...

Armani Suit looked at his two captives. "Still silent?" he asked Billy. He turned his attention to Fred. "Papa here is a traitor, little sister. He dared to turn on his family because he saw a meeting he shouldn't'a seen. Couldn't handle it. Isn't that right, Papa?"

Billy just gazed at Suit.

"What are you talking about?" Fred asked.

"You see, ol' Papa here walked in on a meeting where my organization was acquiring another, with a few not-unexpected consequences. He wasted no time reporting us to the cops. And old Papa here got put into Witness Protection so we couldn't find him to pay 'em back for his betrayal. He cost me, and several of my lieutenants, some time behind bars, which cost my organization quite a bit of capital. I promised him after the verdict that he'd pay me back for any lost years with his own... and I'm here to collect."

Fred looked at Billy, and then back at Suit. "What? What do you mean? You're going to kill Billy? You can't kill him!"

Suit smiled. "You got it all wrong, little sister. I'm gonna kill him," he said as he pointed first at Billy, then at her, "and you're gonna follow."

Spy brought his car to a stop a hundred feet away from the rear of the dry-cleaning shop. Regular police cars and SWAT vans were parked nearby, with police and snipers aiming their weapons at the back door. He activated a screen on his liquid crystal display dashboard, then pressed a virtual button below the image. A single projectile fired from the car's front grill and impacted a utility pole on the opposite side of the intersection, past the front of the shop. A small cylinder rotated on the shaft until it stopped with a small lens facing the shop. Spy saw on his dashboard monitor the police cars flanking the front of the store.

He looked through the one-way windshield and windows of his car to survey the buildings around the shop, the traffic movements, non-existent pedestrian traffic, and made his plan. He waited for the moving cars to clear away from the street, then got out of his car and disappeared into the twilight shadows...

Darkness overtook the city streets, and the black of night was broken only by a couple cones of light created by the evenly-spaced street lights. The rear of Billy's shop was darker, as the light above the back door was disintegrated in the earlier explosion that blew in the door. The SWAT officers had to switch to night-vision scopes, and the regular police officers pulled back so as not to get caught in any potential night-time cross-fire.

A SWAT sniper was gazing at the shop's back door when what looked like a dark blur passed through his field of vision. That glance did not tell him if the blur was a person or bird or just a random night shadow, as there was no other movement detected after. Regardless, he said into his active boom mike by his mouth, "Twelve here. I thought I saw a shape or something move. Can anyone confirm?"

"Ten here. Cannot confirm."

"Thirteen. No movement from my angle."

"Fourteen. No movement seen."

"Twelve.10-4." He rubbed his eyes quickly and went back to gazing through his rifle lens...

◆◆◆

One of the Asians brought a chair from the lobby and set it before an open cabinet that held containers of various dry-cleaning chemicals. Suit sat and faced his prisoners. "If you're going to kill us," Billy said, "what are you waiting for?"

"Ah, Papa finally speaks!" said Suit. "Excellent! I do truly wish your death to be on a friendly note. After all, we have a couple matters to conclude."

"There's nothing to discuss," said Billy. "You murdered those people in cold blood. I couldn't care less what you thought you were doing, you deserved to be arrested, tried, and jailed."

"It was business, Papa, and none of YOUR damned business." Suit smiled as he leaned back on the two rear chair legs. Another Asian glanced down at Fred's desk for the first time and saw the small picture frame of Fred and her daughter. He handed it to Suit. "What's this? You have a kid?"

Fred glared at him through teary eyes.

"You don't have to worry about her, she'll join you after we conclude our business here. Now, as to why we're waiting? No chance of some random passerby hearing or seeing anything going on in here through the front. You do have a very open-air business here, Papa. Well done."

"Why does he keep calling you 'Papa', Billy?" Fred asked.

"That's what my kids called me when I worked for him," Billy said. "I treated them all with respect, like they were my own children."

"You took care of OUR kids," said Suit. "We trusted

you with our kids, and you go and betray us and leave 'em all social orphans."

Billy glared at him. "They are all fatherless because of your own actions, not mine."

Suit laughed. "Semantics. We will collect our debt... and unfortunately, young lady, you will have to join him because you know him, and you know what we look like. Business, you understand..."

"You won't get away with this," said Billy. "You gotta know by now this place has to be surrounded by the cops. Not like you can blow something up here and not get some attention."

Suit guffawed. "You think I don't know about your basement here? And your access to a tunnel system down there?"

"How—?"

Suit leaned close to Billy's face. "Remember that temp you hired 'bout a month back when this little girl was sick? That was one of my boys, scouting the place good when you did your errands."

Billy hung his head. "Damn. Didn't even see it."

"So, you see, I been plannin' this just a bit, as soon as I heard where you was." Suddenly, one of the Asians flew through the air into the office from the hall, hit the wall with the back of his head and neck, and dropped to the floor, unmoving. Suit jumped to his feet. "Kim! What the hell?"

The other Asian flew through the air, hit the same spot, and crumpled to the floor on top of his partner.

Immediately Suit pulled a gun from his belt and stepped to Billy, grabbed him by the neck, pulled him out of the chair and back across the room to the chemical cabinet, holding him in front to guard himself. The guards he had watching the hole where the back door was blown in, and the front lobby, followed in succession through the air into the office. "Whoever you are, I have a hostage! I'll blow his brains all over this room if you don't show yourself!" Fred involuntarily gasped as she watched a muscular solid-black figure slowly step into the office and move to her side. In his hand he held his .45 automatic, pointed at the floor.

"And just what the hell you supposed to be? You some kinda cop or something?"

"Something," the haunting electronic base voice replied.

Suit smiled. "Cute. Smartass answer. I like that." He looked at the gun in Spy's hand. "I don't suppose I can ask you politely to toss me that nice-lookin' piece, can I?"

"You can ask."

Suit laughed, never moving his pistol from Billy's head. "Well, I'll say this, you're good. No one ever busted all my boys like that before. What are you? SWAT? Homeland Security?"

"Something," Spy said again.

Suit's eyes widened as he said mockingly, "OOO, you scare me! You think you Bruce Willis or some big action star like that?"

This time Spy said nothing. Behind his black lenses he studied the chemical containers behind Suit and Billy. His gaze focused on the container labeled "hydrocarbon" behind and just to the side of Suit's head.

"Well, this has not gone as I planned," said Suit. "So we'll have to do this the old-fashioned way. I want a fast car delivered to the back door, and me and Papa here are gonna go for a ride... or he dies now."

Spy cocked his head as he said, "We're shelving this discussion. You can't blast your way out the way you came in. Don't think you can roll away in a stolen car that easy, either." Spy raised his gun and pointed it at Suit's head. "Why don't you be a good boy and surrender, and everyone can have a Merry Christmas without any bloodshed?"

"You funny! I'm holding the cards here, mystery man, and I'm givin' the orders. So get me a car and move your ass before I decide to take out ol' Papa here and now."

"You're going to kill him anyway. Why wait?" Spy asked. "Oh, right, you need a hostage to get away."

"You pretty smart for a masked man. Tell you what; maybe I let Papa live if you help get me out of here, 'cause I know that's the only way I'm going."

Without warning, Spy moved his hand to the right and fired at the hydrocarbon container that was now directly behind Suit's head, which also shielded Billy from the small blast.

Suit never felt the explosion that consumed him...

Spy had no way of knowing how much of the volatile chemical was in the container, so he had simply hoped for the best when he fired. He was slightly surprised when he roused himself from the rubble of the office and the clock in the top view of his computer lenses told him he'd been unconscious for only a few seconds. He felt something long and hard on the length of his back; he reached behind him and rolled the coat rack off his back. He looked over at Billy with the smoking body of Suit on his back, who looked back and nodded as he freed himself of the corpse. Fred rolled her head to the side to face Spy and smiled before breaking out into laughter.

The masked agent was caught off-guard. "What's so funny, miss?" he asked gently.

Billy could only smile as he tried not to laugh himself. A red scarf draped across the agent's back and areas of white sheetrock dusted the mask's jaw area and a large spot on the side of the head. The holiday image broke the tension of them both having nearly just been killed. Finally, Billy started laughing with her. Spy got to his knees, and the scarf slid off his back and to the floor behind him. His black uniform was covered in sheetrock dust, but he didn't acknowledge it, if he even noticed yet.

Spy rose to his feet, looked around the rubble for his dropped gun, eventually finding it by Fred's overturned desk. After he clipped it to its slat, he removed a knife from the scabbard behind the slat and freed Billy and Fred. They all heard voices from the back of police calling "clear" as they entered the building. They had started advancing when they heard Spy's explosion from outside. "Are you both alright?" he asked them.

Billy and Fred looked at each other. "Yeah," he said, "we're fi—" he looked up to an empty room, which was quickly filled with SWAT and regular uniformed officers. One stopped at the office entrance, his rifle pointed at the two, then noticing the four bodied against the wall. "You two okay?"

"Yeah," Billy nodded. "Yeah..."

The next day, while Billy was out front surveying the damage to his shop, a white Mercedes convertible pulled to a stop beside him. A nicely-curved redhead got out of the car, her crimson dress darker than but a perfect complement to her natural red locks. She approached Billy with her right hand extended. "Mister Lawrence? My name is Jan Jason, executive vice-president for Jason Enterprises in Richmond." She paused to look at the cracked and broken front plate-glass windows from Spy's explosion. "Wow.

Quite a bit of damage here. Insurance going to help you?"

"No idea," said Billy.

She looked at him. "Are you okay?"

"Yeah."

"You don't look it."

"Miss Jason—"

"Mrs.," she corrected politely.

"I'm sorry. Mrs. Jason, I have no idea what you want with me right now, but I'm not the one to be concerned about. My assistant, Fred... she doesn't have insurance, and this event has caused her a lot of medical bills just for getting checked out at the hospital, and her daughter's in foster care right now until her mom is out of the hospital..."

"Mister Lawrence... Billy. I'm here to let you know I'm here to help, if you'll let me."

He turned to her. "Why would you? I'm just a little shop owner—"

Jan smiled at him. "We have a…friend…in common. Likes to wear all-black." His eyes widened. "He said you might need a little help."

Billy was still stunned from watching his mystery hero last night. "I'm going to be relocated... I mean, I have to relocate."

Jan crossed her arms below her breasts. "Do you like it here, Billy?"

Billy nodded.

"Well, our friend in black is taking care of everything for you right now..."

Xander Chamberlain ran one of the competing cartels in New York. He'd been expanding his cartel since taking over when Papa caused his predecessor to be jailed so many years before. Xander was enjoying a steaming cup of tea in his spacious study when there was a loud THUMP behind his chair.

He leapt from his chair dropping his tea cup, and turned to face Spy pointing a gun at him, Suit's burnt body at his feet. "Who are you?" Xander demanded, holding his nose from the aroma. "How did you get in here?"

The black-clad agent replied, "This is what happens when you send anyone after Papa. The other four are in police custody." He stepped forward until his black lenses were inches from Xander's own eyes. "Unless you care to join your friend here in eternal slumber, I suggest your organization forget all about Papa." He raised his .45 and pushed the barrel against Xander's left eye. "If I have to come back here, you will be the first one to die. Have I made myself clear?"

Xander carefully nodded.

Spy lowered his gun and stepped to the side, giving Xander a clear view of Suit's body. "How did you get him in here—?" He turned to face him, but the dark figure was already gone...

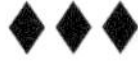

ONE YEAR LATER
CHRISTMAS EVE

Billy dabbed his napkin to his lips, then placed it on the table next to his empty dinner plate. "That was delicious, Fred," he said, a happy smile on his face.

Anna finished her glass of milk. "Can we open a present now? Just one?"

Fred stacked their emptied plates and gathered their silverware. "No, baby girl, presents in the morning. But you can go start the 'Charlie Brown Christmas' DVD while I finish cleaning up dinner."

"Okay!" the girl said happily, running into the living room.

Billy gathered the paper napkins and glasses and followed Fred into the kitchen. He stepped behind her and wrapped his arms around her waist. She rested her hands on his arms and laid her head back on his chest. "Merry Christmas, sweetheart," she said to him.

He kissed the top of her head. "Merry Christmas, my love." He released her and resumed helping clean up. He tied up the garbage bag in the trash can, saying, "I'll take this out, be right back."

"Okay."

Without turning on the light, Billy stepped out the back door of the small house to the herbie-curbie at the back end of the driveway.

"Looks like all's well, Papa."

Billy jumped at the sound of the familiar electronic deep bass as he dropped the garbage bag. "It's you!" he said to his mystery hero, who was hidden in the shadows of the night. "I wondered if I'd ever see you again."

"I don't normally make return visits anywhere," Spy said, "but I had to bring you updated information."

"Can you sit?" Billy asked as he gestured to the picnic table. He almost gasped as he saw the mystery man already seated. "You do seem to come and go."

"Ancient Chinese Secret," Spy said. He waited for Billy to sit across from him. "Mister Chamberlain required a couple more visits to convince him leaving you alone was in his best interest, both personally and financially. And from what I see here, you've come a long way the past year. It's good to see you happy."

"I am. Due in no small part to you, saving my life last year... saving both our lives."

Spy crossed his arms on the table and leaned forward. "Does she know?"

"Fred? Yeah, I got the okay from my handler. But I don't understand just who you are, and why you're interested in me."

"You're a Purple Heart recipient and single-handedly caught one of the most-wanted Al-Qaida leaders in Iraq. You just happened to be in the wrong place at the wrong time here, and you don't deserve to spend the rest of your life looking over your shoulder." He nodded at the house. "When I saw you two last year it was obvious that she had feelings for you. And I saw you felt the same way...but I knew why you couldn't let her get close. Mrs. Jason promised you last year that you'd be safe. I'm here to keep that promise. You'll never have to look over your shoulder again. You're a free man, Cory Mendle."

Billy smiled. "I haven't heard that name in years. Didn't even sound familiar when I told Fred the truth back in January. If it's all the same, I'm Billy Lawrence now." He looked at the back door. "I proposed back in August. But that flood in September destroyed their house on the other side of town, so they moved in with me a little earlier than planned. It's tight, but we're happy. I'd like to invite you to the wedding but I don't know where to send the invitation." He looked back at Spy... who was gone.

On the tabletop in his place was a large manila envelope.

Fred came out the back door. "I thought I heard you talking to someone out here, darling."

"I was," Billy admitted. "With our mysterious hero."

Fred sat down next to him. "Oh, my! Did you get his name? I'd so love to thank him properly for saving us... and helping us find each other."

"I asked...but he just disappeared, like he did last year. He left this." He pointed at the envelope.

She picked it up and asked, "May I?" Billy nodded, and she opened it. Inside were folded piece of paper and a regular number 10 envelope. She unfolded the paper and gasped. "Billy! It's a title to a house!" He looked at it in her hands and the address listed. "You know where this is, Billy?" She looked at the title again. "And it's in your name! Did the man just give us a house?"

"I don't know," said Billy. "What's in the envelope?"

She opened it and nearly slid to the patio deck in shock. She handed him the bank draft. "One million dollars?" he gasped.

"Who is it from?" she asked, shocked.

"No one listed," he said, staring at the draft.

Anna came out the back door and ran to Billy and Fred. "Whatcha got, Mommy? Uncle Billy?"

Billy picked her up in one arm and put his other around Fred, kissing them both on the head. "A miracle, Anna. An actual Christmas miracle..."

35

REAL TO REEL MURDER

Christina Gray ran into the bathroom, slammed and locked the door behind her, and turned off the light. Panicked and gasping for air, she made her way to the corner of the room and crouched between the toilet and the wall. Tears had smudged her makeup, her clothes were disheveled, and lengthy locks of blonde hair stuck to her face. She held tightly to a long kitchen knife covered in blood.

Slow, heavy footsteps advanced down the hallway, drawing nearer to the bathroom. Light from the hallway glowed inward a few inches under the door, but was quickly shadowed by the man's feet when he stopped just outside.

Christina gasped, squeezing a hand over her mouth when the doorknob jiggled. The sound of her heartbeat pounded in her ears...the doorknob rattled louder and her eyes widened. The shadow moved away, and uninterrupted light crept in under the door once again. For a few seconds there was silence, no footsteps, no sound at all. The light in the hallway went out, and Christina tightened her grip on the knife handle. Fear grabbed her by the throat and beads of sweat trickled down her forehead. Her foreboding dread was palpable, waiting for the unknown.

The silence was broken when the door crashed open, splinters flying in all directions. Instinctively, Christina screamed out in the darkness...

"CUT!" the director yelled. Studio lights flared on one by one, ending the eerie scene of the latest Hollywood horror TV episode. "That's a print," Director Zane Kendril said happily. "Reset for Brian's close-up."

Staging employees scattered about, murmuring amongst themselves while they proceeded with various assignments. Harri Lewis, the makeup director for the episode, came forward. She and her crew touched up the face of the episode's villain, played by actor Brian Towers. "We need some fresh blood lines to mimic him getting cut from smashing through the door," ordered the five-foot-two director. The cinematographer moved the camera for a floor-level shot.

Garrett Crenshaw, assistant to Bethany Heyward, who was portraying the character "Christine", came forward, opening a light robe to cover her shoulders. The studio was chilly for the shoot, and she shivered. Her wardrobe was moist; it was necessary for the scene. She approached Harri. "Great makeup and practicals, Harri. It seemed so real!"

Harri smiled. "If you believe it on set, the viewers will eat it up in their living rooms."

Twenty minutes later Zane yelled, "Action!" and watched the monitor. The camera followed Brian crashing through the door while hidden stage grips dropped pieces of wood-colored Styrofoam around him. Brian turned his head to his right, furrowed his brow, and furled his lips back into an evil clench with his teeth.

"Cut!" Zane snapped. "Reset. Brian let's be a little more pissed off this time, okay? You just smashed through a damned door to get at her. Bethany! Come back, please! When I say action, give me a scream for him to react to."

"You got it," said Bethany. She took a drink from her water bottle and moved back to the set, out of sight of the camera.

Harri and crew reset the makeup and brown-grain foam pieces. The director yelled "Action!" and the scene repeated. This time Zane bellowed and threw his arms in the air, declaring, "Print! Call it a night, everyone!" The makeup director sat back in her studio chair and sighed. "You okay, Harri?"

"I'm about outa blood, Zane."

He looked at the squeeze bottle of red liquid in her hand. "Still looks full."

"No," she chuckled. "In me, Zane. In me." She closed her eyes and laid her head back for a minute before beginning cleanup for the night.

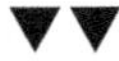

Harri sat at the drawing table in her home office, reading the shooting script for the next day and making sketches of character makeup and practical effects, trying to rely on computer-generated images as little as possible.

Her roommate and best friend Elise DeVeaux knocked gently on the open office door. "Busy, Harri?" she asked softly, her voice still carrying a slight slur from a lifetime of deafness. She was cured to a point through special surgery and state-of-the-art hearing aids. A speech therapist worked with her weekly, but Elise knew she'd never really speak like other people.

The short blond artist sat back in her chair and stretched her arms outward. "Yeah, but I could use a break," she replied. "Zane wanted a redesign for the big murder scene, and I have to say I agree with his vision."

"I've enjoyed watching you on the set," said Elise. "I had no idea how much work you do, besides your secret agent stuff. It's fascinating to see all the cameras and people, then see what it looks like on a TV."

Harri tapped at the script on her draft board. "This is how it all really begins. Someone has to write it." She picked up the script and offered it to Elise.

"Wow! I barely understand all this. This becomes a TV show?" she asked as she flipped through the pages.

The police scanner, redesigned and modified to receive encrypted channels, squawked beside Harri's drawing table. "...10-31 in progress..."

"What's that?" Elise asked.

"Break-in," said Harri.

Elise opened the wardrobe beside the door and reached in. She removed a black leather gun belt with a flat metal buckle. "Do you need to go?" she asked innocently.

"Nah," Harri answered, shaking her head gently. "Remember, stuff like this is for the locals...not the Feds. Besides, I got a script to finish reviewing. I'm just hoping the Task Force doesn't call me in for something before the end of this shoot." She looked at the clock beside the bureau. "Wow, didn't realize the time. Wanna go get something to eat?"

"Sure! Can we get Italian again?"

Harri nodded. "Whatever you want..."

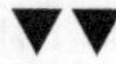

The Italian restaurant was fully decked out in Christmas decorations and lights, creating a festive mood for its diners. Harri and Elise had just finished their salads when the main courses were delivered.

"I love spaghetti!" Elise said when the waitress set the plate on the table, with garlic bread to the side.

"I still can't believe you never had spaghetti growing up," said Harri.

"Yeah, I know. Father was so strict about our meals. Nothing except American."

Harri harrumphed at Elise's words, remembering how Elise's father had abused her for years.

Elise took a sip of her Sangiovese. "Mmm! This is delicious, especially with the spaghetti!"

Harri sipped from her glass and sighed. "I love good Chianti, but that can get really expensive."

"Harri," Elise said as she set her glass down, "thank you so much for introducing me to things like this. The food, the wine, and so many other things that I had no idea even existed."

"My pleasure, Elise. Glad I could be your friend."

"You're my best friend! So… what do I do now?"

Harri looked at her quizzically. "What do you mean?"

"Well," she replied, "what am I supposed to do now that your TV job takes you away more often…or your Task Force job takes you even further?"

Harri savored her mouthful of lasagna before answering. "That's kinda up to you, Elise. You're under the Task Force Division's sponsorship, so you're really free to do whatever you want. Learn, explore, study…it's all up to your imagination and desire."

"How did you become an agent?"

Harri looked at her again, this time with raised eyebrows. "You know I can't tell you that," she said, smiling.

"Doesn't hurt to keep asking." They both laughed. "Come on, I'm already part of your secret organization anyway…why can't you tell me?"

"You're getting real good at this whole logic thing. Okay, you win." She sipped her wine again. "When I was in the academy, I really wanted to study and get into military intelligence. Okay, I admit I loved James Bond."

"Who?"

The agent smiled and shook her head. "Boy, have we got a movie marathon coming up. Anyway, my thesis was on a new approach toward stealth technology in personal equipment to give our ground military better cover from enemy heat sensors and such. Got the highest grade in my class, plus special commendations for conceptual proposals. So, while I was on duty in Iraq there was a plan put forth for infiltrating al-Qaida compounds a few klicks away. I made some suggestions for our men going in, including some quick facial disguises for, well, let's just say for *special* reasons. The mission was a success, no one lost or even injured. A month after returning stateside I got a visit from two men who identified themselves as specialized Federal Task Force Division. Long story short, they asked if I wanted to serve my country with the best of the best. I didn't even think. I said, 'Why the hell not?'"

Elise laughed.

"What?"

"You're so cute when you cuss!"

Harri blushed. "That's the strangest compliment I've ever gotten, thank you. Anyway, I reported to Task Force and went through the training process to become its new

Agent Proteus, master of disguise and camouflage. Went through a whole lot more training, too."

"So why do you do Hollywood shows? You already make lots of money with Task Force?"

"True, I do. When every mission is one you may not come back from, you get paid a lotta money to make it worth the danger. But I like to work on the sets to keep honing my special effects skills. It's not like I'm a character in a TV show or novel, where every week or every book I'm in a new life-threatening death trap, so I have time to kill… so why not have fun and practice my art in the process?"

Elise swirled spaghetti noodles around her fork. "So, what's your day look like tomorrow?"

"I have to be in by 3:00 in the morning to start prepping the makeup and prosthetics for the actors, first call's at 7:00, then I'm on set all day for touch up and resets for the last two scenes of the episode."

"All day for two scenes?"

"Yup. All day for what amounts to just a few minutes on the TV screen."

"But, Harri, it's almost Christmas! Why are you doing a scary episode this time of year? You should be doing Christmas shows!"

Harri laughed. "We did the Christmas episodes back in July, remember?"

"Oh… I remember now. Sorry. Just seems weird to make Christmas shows in the summer."

"That's Hollywood for ya. The Christmas shows have to shoot in summer so all the editing and post production and such can be finished, then handed off to the marketing folks to make the commercials and ads for TV Guide and magazines for December issues."

"So, what're you shooting now?"

"It's for next Halloween."

Elise sat back in her seat. "Wow. I wish I could do what you do."

Harri looked at Elise and smiled. "Now that you mention it…"

▼▼

"Zane, I wanna kill my girlfriend."

The director looked at Harri and Elise and laughed. "That's the first time anyone ever said that in Hollywood with a perfect straight face!" He crossed his arms and continued, "Whatcha got in mind?"

"Well, you've got extras coming in as dead victims; let me add one to the mix? She's so new to all this, I thought I'd give her an early birthday present...a small part...if that's okay with you."

"Oh? When's your birthday, Elise?"

"January 2nd."

Zane made a downturned smile, contemplating, and then nodded. "Have at it then, Harri. Elise, I hope you enjoy your day playing a corpse! We'll do the paperwork later. Hey, Top, I want that angle sharp and tight." Zane walked off to discuss the scene setup with the cinematographer, leaving the two women to think and speculate.

"Paperwork?" Elise asked.

"You're gonna get paid to be dead, girlfriend," Harri said with a knowing grin.

Elise thought about it for a second, then replied, "Wow!"

Harri led her to the makeup center and called to a young man wearing a set-access lanyard. "Cam! I need another set of wardrobe for a new victim!"

"Got it!" Cam replied, scurrying off the set.

"So, what do I do?" Elise asked nervously.

"Well, first you're gonna have to get naked so we can dress you in clothes that can get bloody."

"WHAT?"

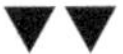

Elise was dressed in a simple blue dress and black flats. Lights and mirrors in the dressing room glowed, accenting every facial feature. Harri settled her into a makeup chair. "First, I'm gonna base you to make you look like you just had a traumatic death." She applied some smudges to Elise's forehead and cheeks, and then turned to a tray of pre-made skin appliances. Harri selected one long piece and placed it against Elise' throat. "I think I'm gonna make you dead from having your neck sliced open," she said.

"Gross, Harri! How can you do this stuff?" Elise shuttered for a moment, then calmed and smiled. "That's a scary thought, but also kind of fun."

"Just don't move while I get this on, especially no talking until it's glued in place, ok?"

Elise nodded. Harri smiled while she began applying the prosthetic to her neck. She finished the top edge, aware of someone approaching their station. "Hey, Harri, let's give your friend a real present. Can you rig her to spurt?" Zane asked.

Elise looked up in a nervous wide-eyed surprise as Harri replied, "Sure. What's up boss?"

Zane winked at Harri. "Elise, I'm gonna let you die on camera."

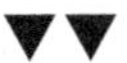

Harri and Zane were positioning everyone on the set for the take. They'd already recorded her being "chased" by the killer, close-ups of her reacting to the impending knife thrust, and were readying her for her death scene. Elise was nervous, having never been in an environment as an actor before in all her visits to Harri's sets. Her back faced the cameras, and her front was wired and tubed to make an explosion of fake blood gushing from her throat and down the front of her body when the killer sliced her neck.

"Now, you ready for this, Elise?"

"Yes, sir, it's pretty yuck and scary...but I'm okay," she replied.

Zane looked at Elise and said, "Harri, she's way over nervous. Fix it! And I can see her hearing aids again. Cover them a little more." Harri looked at her tablet to see how Elise looked in what would be the moment immediately preceding the scene.

"Crap...thought I had all that covered," she said aloud. Harri moved Elise's hair just enough to cover her hearing aids. "Okay, baby, relax. Everything is perfect, you look fantastic, and I can't wait to see you on TV! Okay, looks good. Brian, in place!" Brian followed Harri's order and moved to Elise's side, held out the hand with the "murder weapon" knife and stepped back beyond arm's length.

"Why so far back?" Elise asked.

"Camera trick," Harri said, crouched beside Elise. "Oldest one in the book; when he swings the knife at you he'll actually be almost a foot away, but the camera angle will make it look like he's right on top of you at that moment. Just remember, you're gonna feel just a little surge when this tube blows and you're gonna get covered. Remember Zane's directions, okay? It's not real, hon. it's all fake. It's not a real knife or blood, okay?"

"Okay, Harri. I'll do okay, I hope. It's just, well, you know. My father and all. The things he did to us. It seems to keep coming up and I sort of panic. I'll do my best."

Zane's voice barked before Harri and Elise finished talking. "All right, clear the set," Zane ordered. He sat in his chair to view the scene on a monitor while the camera recorded. "Quiet! And… action!"

Brian growled and made a swing with his knife toward Elise' throat. The sensor Harri put in the blade caused a small charge in the tube on Elise' neck to explode at that precise second, sending a spurt of red blood-like fluid flying away from her neck and flowing down her dress. She dropped to her knees, as rehearsed, and finally to her back. The blood flowed down her neck and onto the stage floor.

"CUT!" Zane called out. Happily, he jumped out of his chair. "That was awesome! That's a print! Reset for Bethany's murder!" He turned to Elise and said with a big smile, "You were incredible! Best death I've ever directed!" He winked at her and moved to prepare for the next shoot.

Harri helped Elise to her feet. "I'm a mess!" Elise said.

"Yeah, but now you're a messy star!" Harri replied. "Let's get you cleaned up…"

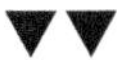

Bethany arrived on-set early to prepare for the day's shoot; mainly comprised of close-ups. On prior days there were the shots of her running into the bathroom, hiding beside the toilet, running back out after the killer breaks through the door. On close-up days she always preferred to be alone on the set to begin "getting into character", feeling the isolation without another soul in sight, pulling it into her mind...feeling her past life jump into play.

There was no dialogue in the shooting schedule, it was all reaction shots. She loved reaction days because she could put all her energy into speaking volumes with glances and breaths, and loved the particular challenge.

Standing at the bathroom doorway; a new breakaway door had been hung prior to the camera recording, so she pretended to grab the doorknob to open it. Bethany took a few fast breaths to get into the mood, then acted like the frightened Christina trying to hide from her pursuer.

"Oh, right, forgot I was carrying the knife, damn," she said to herself. She reposed herself with one hand clenched, "holding" the fake knife and the other hand opening the door. She hyperventilated again, then swung open the door to run into the bathroom. She fled to the corner beside the toilet and crouched down; her arm rose "holding" the knife. She made herself jump as she imagined the door being broken in. "That sucks. I gotta talk with Harri about doing something to make me jump instinctively to make this look perfect."

There was a metallic bang which echoed across the soundstage. "Hello?" Bethany called out. No one answered. She looked at her watch; it was almost time for the early crew to begin arriving, including Harri to do her and Brian's makeup. "Anyone there?"

When there was no answer, she dismissed it as just another mysterious sound in a decades-old building, as she'd heard many times before. She turned her attention back to her character prep.

Garrett approached the set. "Good morning, Bethany," he said happily. Startled, she jumped slightly.

"Garrett, you scared me."

"Last day on this episode! I brought you a chocolate mocha as always, plus a couple cheese Danishes."

Bethany smiled. "Thank you, Garrett. Didn't you hear me say hello?"

"Sorry, I had my keys in my mouth with my hands full. Didn't mean to scare you."

She smiled at him. "That's okay. Would you mind setting them at Harri's table? She should be here any time."

"Sure thing." He left her alone on the bathroom set.

"I'm going to practice my terror screams," she called back, "so don't worry!"

"It'll be music to my ears!" he returned.

"Let me know how it sounds, okay? I'm striving for real terror."

"You got it."

He was at Harri's makeup chair when he heard Bethany call out, "Here goes…" a loud scream followed.

"Uh, kind of lifeless," Garrett said. "Give it another try."

Harri entered the studio door just as Bethany let out her second scream, making her pause. Realizing it was Bethany rehearsing, she walked to her station. "Hey, Beth, not bad!" she chimed in. "Suck in deeper and push out with your diaphragm more."

"That you, Harri?" Bethany said from staged bathroom. "Good idea, thanks! Here goes—"

"Wait!" said Harri. "I know there's no dialogue, but pretend you have something to say to lead into it. In fact," Harri said as she hooked her makeup belt around her waist, "let me do a quick base to accent your scream face."

Bethany laughed. "Only you can say something like that with a straight face and make it sound normal."

She sat patiently on the floor while Harri pulled a

compact from her belt and lightly dusted Bethany's face. "Just a little trick of mine to help me make particular, um, creases stand out more in the close-up shots." She put the compact back and stepped away. "I'll leave you to your screams now."

"Thank you, Harri." When Harri was out of eyesight Bethany closed her eyes and played the scene in her mind…

Brian was already at Harri's table for his makeup. "Cam's gonna do you today, Bri," Harri said. "She should be here any minute now."

Bethany screamed.

"Sounds better, Beth!" Harri called out.

"Well, I'm gonna go take a pee while I have a minute," said Brian. He looked at the mocha and Danishes awaiting Bethany. "Wish my assistant did that."

"Maybe if you quit asking her out?" Harri mused under her breath.

"Ha, ha," Brian said as he walked off to the real bathrooms opposite the bathroom set.

Bethany screamed.

"Better!" Harri said.

"Did you know," Garrett asked Harri, "that Zane wants to turn this into a two-parter? He talked with Bethany's agent and the writer to let her character survive this episode and be in the next."

Harri looked at him. "What? They picked a helluva time to do a rewrite before the last shots of the episode!"

Bethany screamed.

"Bethany, you sound like a girl!" Brian yelled from the bathroom.

"I am a girl, you asshole!" she shouted back.

"I wouldn't know," he replied as he exited the restroom.

"In your dreams," she returned. "And I didn't hear you wash your hands by the way."

Harri smiled. "That sounds like the worst dialogue ever."

"They've done other shows together," Garrett laughed and shrugged his shoulders. "Writers and producers like their chemistry, keep putting them together as 'special guest stars'. They make for ratings."

"They are good." Harri opened her shooting folio. "Shit. I didn't realize that the close-ups are out of order for the day. That's what I get for doing my final notes after an Italian dinner."

"Too much Chianti again, girl?"

"Very funny. She's right, you're an asshole."

Bethany screamed once more.

Harri continued, "I've got to clean her up twice today between close-up shots. I hate that! Oh well…"

"Is there any coffee?" Brian yelled.

Harri sniffed the air. "I think an assistant just arrived and started a pot!"

"Good! I'd hate to think I smelled like caffeine!"

Garrett winced. "And now my desire for coffee is gone for the day."

Bethany screamed again.

"Don't use it up, Beth!" Harri called out. "Cameras roll soon."

Latoya Geller, an intern on set, called from the service table, "Hi-test will be ready in a couple!"

"I'll be just a minute!" Brian yelled.

Bethany screamed one more time.

"She's got a great set of lungs," said Latoya as she crossed the stage to the bathroom.

"Don't say things like that," said Garrett, "she

doesn't want to get a reputation as a 'scream queen'."

"She's got nothing to worry about," said Harri. "She's good, but I've heard better on the big screen. Hey, Beth, whenever you run out of air come on over so I can get started."

"Harri!" called Zane as he entered the set from the bathrooms. "How's my favorite gusher?" He gave the short woman a tight hug.

"Always ready to gross you out," she replied in his arms. "Too bad there's no gushing today. Just drips and smudges."

"We could always do a rewrite first thing."

"We're coming up on the Christmas holidays," said Harri, breaking away from his arms. "You really want to ruin your reputation as the friendliest director on TV? And how'd you sneak in without us seeing you?"

Zane laughed. "I have a key to the back door. Hey, we're shooting a horror script three weeks before Christmas. Anyone see the paradox here?"

Brian sat down in his makeup chair. "Ain't that two physicians on a golf course?"

Harri groaned. "How do you always show up with that terrible pun whenever anyone says the word 'paradox'?"

"What can I say, Harri, it's a gift."

Cam arrived. "Sorry I'm late, everyone. Traffic accident. I'll be ready to make you messy in just a couple, Brian."

He craned his neck around toward the intern, "No sweat, gives me time for a cup of coffee… if any is ready?"

"Coming right up!" Latoya said as she brought him a cup from the service table.

He took a sip and sighed. "Now that's a damn fine cuppa coffee."

"Wrong show," Harri quipped. She realized Bethany hadn't screamed in several minutes and hadn't come to the makeup chair either. "Beth? You okay?"

Silence was the reply.

"Beth?" Harri called louder. Still no reply. She instinctively reached for where her Beretta would have been holstered in her Task Force uniform, but instead only touched her makeup pouch. "Zane, come with me," she said, nearly an order rather than a request.

Zane followed Harri's uncharacteristic commanding voice.

She led him to the set where Bethany had been rehearsing; she was sitting on the floor beside the toilet—

—a large knife protruding from her chest, blood pooling around where she sat.

"Holy shit," Harri said...

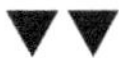

Detectives examined the murder scene while the uniformed officers spoke separately with Zane and Harri and everyone who was in the soundstage at the time of the murder. Everyone else was kept out.

"There was only about four minutes after the last time we heard her do a rehearsal scream until when Zane and I found her," Harri told one officer, and repeated the same thing to a detective several minutes later.

"Thank you," said the detective as he handed her a card. "If you think of anything else, please give me a call any time."

"Detective," she said, "what do you make of it?"

"Well, there's nothing that indicates motive so far, and no clue to who did it, but we're only just beginning our investigation."

"Please let me know if you find anything, too, okay?" she asked.

"Of course." He stepped away.

Harri looked over at Brian. He held his head in his hands, tears rolling down his cheeks. He and Bethany had been a Hollywood couple on-screen only, and she knew he was hurting. The detective interviewing him finally stepped away, giving her the opportunity to go to his side. "How you doin', Bri?"

"I—I can't believe it," he said, his voice shaky. "Why?"

"That's what I intend to find out."

He looked at the makeup artist. "You? What can you do?"

Harri smiled. "I meant them, the detectives. They'll figure it out." *And once they get outta here I can get to work myself...*

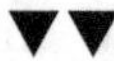

Elise knocked on Harri's office door in their apartment and stepped in unbidden. She found Harri dressed in her form-fitting black Task Force uniform, matching knee-high leather boots, and locking her black leather gun belt around her hips. The flat metal buckle plate was inscribed with two upside-down equilateral triangles. The gun in the holster was a black-plated Beretta. A matching pair of elbow-high leather gloves were draped over the desk chair.

"Oh! You have a case?" Elise asked.

"I'm going to investigate a murder," Harri replied, slipping on the gloves. She reached into the open bureau for a pair of black glasses, which were actually an independent computer system operated by voice command or eye movement. "Stay here, girlfriend. Proteus has a job to do."

Elise gave her a hug. "Be safe, Proteus. Let me know when you're coming home. You know I worry."

Harri smiled and stepped over to the second-floor window. She opened the pane and pushed open the screen. When she pressed a button inside the window frame, a hidden panel opened revealing a length of knotted rope that instantly unfurled to the street.

"Harri! You're going out the window? Why?"

"Well, I can't very well let the neighbors see me in this uniform. They're not supposed to know I'm a secret federal agent, remember? Press this button when I'm at the ground, it'll retract automatically."

"Okay, Harri. I don't like it, you could fall. But I understand."

She nodded and lifted herself out the window and slid to the ground.

A Task Force car had been delivered to her apartment building parking lot when she called for one from the local field office on her way home. Having the black sports car added a feeling of safety as she drove back to the studio to conduct her own investigation… with a stop on the way…

Detective Michael Carrington sat at his regular table in the outside patio of a Starbucks in Hollywood, sipping a chocolate mocha while taking a break from his evening shift. The middle-aged man was in good shape, with a full head of black hair yet to be lined with any gray. He wore reading glasses, which were presently on the table next to his steaming coffee, and he watched the evening traffic in both directions, following each car with trained intensity.

"Hey, Mike," said a female voice from behind him.

"Dammit, Proteus!" he sputtered, steadying his hand after nearly knocking his coffee over. "You tryin' ta give me a coronary or somethin'?"

"We both know your heart is perfectly healthy," she said as she sat down. Unlike him, she kept her black glasses on, which served as a mask against him potentially recognizing her.

He looked at the gun on her hip. "You still packin' unnumbered heat, girl?"

"You're welcome to try checking it," she said, smiling.

Mike smiled back. "Well, I guess you're Batmobile is around here somewhere, hero girl. Can't believe I didn't hear it."

"You know you won't, boyfriend."

"So, what do I owe the honor of your return visit tonight? Calling in one of them favors I owe you?"

She leaned forward and interlaced her gloved fingers on the table. "You can call this a debt paid if you want. Whatcha got on the Heyward murder on the soundstage today?"

"Ain't my case, girl. I knows nothing, I hears nothing."

She placed a hand on his forearm. "Aw, c'mon, boyfriend. You can't help a girl out as an early Christmas present?"

"I seen you take down half a dozen bank robbers at once, why do you think I could help you?" He puffed at his cigarette, chuckling more to himself than at her.

"Because I still believe in human contact. Yeah, I

could access the police records with no trouble, I just wanted to be courteous and ask first." She smiled at him.

"You're good, girl, I'll give ya that. But serious, I'm not on the case, but I think Brocker is on it."

"Brocker?!" she said. "On a murder case? I can't believe he ever got a detective's shield."

"Eh," he replied. "Now I didn't tell ya, okay, girl?"

"You got it, Mike." She was about to get up but stopped herself. "May I ask you a question?"

"Ain't that what you secret agent types do?"

"Ha, ha, yeah. Why aren't you home tonight?"

Mike growled under his breath. "Gail and me's split up."

"Shit, Mike! What happened?"

"Caught her cheatin' on me."

"No!" said Proteus. "How—do you need help?"

He rotated in his chair to look at her. "Nah, I got it girl. Listen, though, do me a favor? If you're trackin' down Bethany's killer… catch him for me, okay? She was actually a friend."

"Didn't realize you knew some stars, Mike."

"Yeah. Used to do security detail on her staff for extra cash after she got to be a big star. We used to have drinks at the end of her shooting days." He saw her eyebrow rise above the rim of her black glasses. "Oh, no, I never did anything more than that! I stayed true to Gail…"

"Mike, are you sure about Gail? Anything I can do to help?"

"Nah. We'll work it out. I just needed the time away to clear my head and think."

She got up and leaned forward to kiss him on the cheek. "You be careful, okay? Merry Christmas…"

"Merry Christmas to you, too, girl." Mike looked up

where she should have been standing but she was already gone into the shadows. "Merry Christmas, Proteus, whoever you are…"

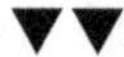

In the soundstage she left the lights off, relying only on the night-vision advantage of her computerized glasses. Picking the locks to get in was no problem for Proteus. Getting around the studio security guards was just as easy. They were fooled by her misdirected sounds outside the gate. But on the soundstage, she made sure not to make any noise.

Proteus slipped under the yellow police tape and began her examination. She went directly to where Bethany's body was found and tapped the side of her glasses to activate the full sensor system.

The spot where her blood pooled was dark, with an outline of where her posterior had been. There was no obvious trail for the police to follow.

The police, however, did not have the advanced technology she did. "Activate 3D scan at micro level." She stared intently at the floor, her lenses magnifying the view at dust-level. While her computer glasses scanned and processed the floor, she thought about how Bethany was positioned and tried to calculate how she was killed.

The hilt of the knife was angled upward from her chest, she recalled, so the thrust had to come from above. She reasoned that the killer was likely standing over her in the corner.

There were fresh disturbances in the minute dust; some she assumed may have been from the medical examiner and her staff removing the body. But if the killer stood over her, Proteus reasoned, then a footstep near the wall may be less disturbed.

She changed her gaze to the baseboard of the bathroom set and saw a mostly-clean footstep in the floor dust that matched what might have been the killer's presumed posture. "Record and extrapolate," she commanded softly. Imagery in her lenses accented the footprint schematic and turned it into a reference base for scanning the entire floor for matching impressions.

Her gaze landed upon a matching print at the bathroom door opening. She went to the doorway and looked left into the set hallway and right toward where the camera would have been set for the doorway close-up; she found a matching impression beside the camera placement marking on the floor. Then she saw another, and another, with the back steps leading toward the bathrooms—

—and the path ended as the disturbances created by the police and detectives destroyed all remaining evidence for her to follow.

"Run diagnostic," she said softly, and she waited as the computer circuitry in her glasses frame processed her command in a link with the more powerful computer system in her car parked nearby.

The readout in her vision indicated that the footprint was of a standard-issue military boot, size eleven, the likely wearer was probably over six feet tall and over two hundred pounds. "Access police records: details on the murder weapon for this location today." She left the soundstage and returned to her car. Once in the car she read the final analysis on the dashboard LCD display.

Records stated it was a common hunting knife, and its description matched the one that was stolen two nights before from a sporting goods store across town. She pressed a virtual button on the dashboard to access the robbery detail to get the store's location...

▼▼

A large piece of plywood covered the opening of the picture window at the Knight Sporting Goods store. Proteus parked her car across the street and ran a system scan of the store from her car's computer. The inside security system was active with infrared beams that rotated in random directions. Within a minute, the computer was able to hone in on the security frequency. She removed a transmitter from her belt pouch and programmed it to the store's security frequency. Exiting the car, her glasses scanned for heat signatures one more time. *Good, no one anywhere around,* she thought. The car door closed automatically and silently.

From the pouch in front of her holster she removed a gun-like tool. Proteus placed it over the deadbolt keyhole first, then the doorknob; she turned the doorknob and the door swung open silently. *Sure do love the tech guys for creating all this cool stuff, makes my job so much easier.*

Once inside, Proteus began surveying the break-in area around the plywood. She smiled as her transmitter turned her entire body invisible to the security system.

Proteus scanned the floor through her glasses, searching for even the minutest of clues. She wasn't surprised when the computer picked up pinhead-size spots of blood amongst the debris. She wondered if the police had seen it and took any of it as evidence. No doubt the thief was cut by a shard of glass. In the upper corner of her glasses a blue dot flashed, informing her that a computer search from her car was complete. "Play," she commanded.

Her view changed to a video from the store's 24-hour security system, the recording now in the database at police headquarters. Watching the video inside her glasses, she saw a man breaking through the front window with an object, perhaps a baseball bat. The window smashed inward. The man flinched, grabbing hold of his right arm with a gloved hand. *Ah, you did get cut,* she thought. Alarms blared. He was only in the store long enough to grab one knife from behind the counter then left through the window opening.

"Rewind. Facial follow."

She viewed the video again, this time closed in on the intruder's face at all times. "Enhance and run facial," she commanded. The video ran again, giving digital enhancements of light and physical embellishments.

A blue dot flashed in her field of vision again. "Show." A face appeared in her right lens. At the same time a red dot flashed to the left. "Excellent." Proteus left, using her tool to relock the door and deadbolt. Once she was in the car, Proteus ordered an address search, and took off into the night…

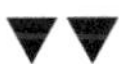

Brian sat in his living room chair, holding a picture of he and Bethany on the set of a movie they had been in the prior summer. They were in swimwear, and the bikini she wore was small, leaving little to the imagination; they were in costume for the movie where they acted as boyfriend/girlfriend in a drama. In the story, his character was dying and she was trying to make his final days happy.

From her car, Proteus' glasses zoomed in. She peered in through the living room window. She saw the photo in one hand…and a .38 special in the other.

His front doorknob exploded from several gunshots. A black-clad form kicked in the door. "On the floor!" she ordered, pointing her weapon at him.

Brian didn't move. His eyes were red and swollen from crying. He simply blinked up at her. "I wondered when someone would show up," he said calmly.

Proteus was taken aback. She knew he couldn't recognize her because of her uniform and glasses. Her blond hair was slicked back. She didn't expect his complete lack of reaction. "Really?"

"Yeah," he replied. "Technology is way too good to expect to get away with anything now. So, how'd you find me?"

"Facial recognition through my special software, plus blood match from a tiny sample recovered from the store and run through our elite database. Why'd you do it, Brian?"

"I fell in love with her, many times over. I tried, asked, pleaded. For years. Nothing worked. She only loved me on camera. She was passionate, real—I could feel it." A tear rolled down his cheek. "She never loved me away from the camera though. She had other men in her real life."

Proteus relaxed her stance slightly. The heat-sensor readings in her lenses allowed her to monitor Brian's body in case he started to do something drastic. "Isn't that how it always is in this town?" she asked.

He chuckled. His grip loosened slightly on the pistol. "More than you know, lady. But we were special. You can see it in any film or show we did together. The magic was there, we were in love!" He stopped for a moment, mouth half-open, before he continued. "We were meant to be together. We were perfect together! Then she had to go and— "

Proteus saw his pulse start to race. "She had to go and what, Brian?"

"She got engaged!" he growled. "Three nights ago she announced her engagement to another man!"

Oh geez, she thought.

"Who are you, anyway?" he demanded. "Is that some kinda uniform? You don't look like a cop."

Proteus opened the front panel of her gun belt buckle and removed a badge which she attached to a fabric strip over her left breast. "Is that better?"

"It doesn't matter anyway..." He took a deep breath and looked at the photo again. "So I killed her. I had to. No one else can have her. Only me. It should have only been me..."

She saw it before he moved raising his gun to shoot, either himself or her. The automatic targeting software in her lens put a bull's eye on his gun and she fired once...sending his gun flying from his hand and across the room. He howled in pain and surprise.

Proteus spun about, her leather boot and hard rubber sole landing aside his face. The impact kicked him out of his chair, sending him crashing through the glass living room table. He lay unconscious on the floor.

She stood over him. "Well, that was easy enough. Now do I take you to jail myself or call in the cops?" She put her gun in her holster. "Oh, what the hell, I got nothing better to do." She grabbed his collar and dragged him outside to her car. "Proteus to Task Force Division. I need a notification sent to the local PD; I'm bringing in a murder suspect...

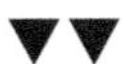

The chief detective at the nearest police station watched as the short blond in the black uniform seemed to effortlessly drag a man twice her size in the front door. When she dropped him at the front desk, he noticed the shield on her uniform. "Oh, sorry, agent," he said without a smile. "We were notified you were bringing in a suspect, we just didn't—"

Proteus smiled. "You didn't expect David to bring in Goliath. I know, I get it all the time." She stood in front of him and looked up into his face, six inches above her own. "And I've taken down more Goliaths than I care to count." She turned to leave.

"Hey, wait, where do you think you're going?"

She stopped and turned back. "In his pants pocket you'll find a complete video file with all the evidence I compiled. You have all the evidence you need for a conviction. My office will be in touch."

He looked down at Brian's unconscious form. "I still need your information for the reports—"

Proteus was already gone.

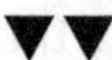

Harri took off her computer glasses and gave them to Elise, who put them back in the bureau. She in turn handed Harri a glass of Pinot Grigio. "You didn't sound too happy when you called," Elise said. "Mission not successful?"

"No, it was successful," Harri replied. "Just unsatisfying." She sat down on the living room couch and rested her booted feet on the coffee table. "It was one of those missions I wish I didn't do."

"Couldn't you have just let the police solve it?"

Harri sipped her wine. "That's the price of being a Task Force agent. Not every mission has a happy ending. And, this one happened on my watch, and I had to solve it quickly…a murder due to the most common and stupidest of reasons…" She sipped again. "But, I'm just the one to make a happy ending anyway…"

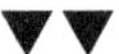

Zane walked onto the soundstage for the first time since the police opened it back up for the director and crew to resume work. He still had the final shots to do for the episode but both his stars were out of the picture now.

"Hey, Zane," he heard Harri say from the shadows.

"Harri," he said. "Nice to see a friendly face first thing."

"I've got something to show you. Wanna join me?"

"Sure." Zane followed Harri to the makeup tables…

…and gasped when he saw Bethany and Brian sitting in their makeup chairs. "What the hell?"

"Zane, this is Barbara and Carl, professional make up models. I used the life casts I made of Beth and Bri some time and created lifelike masks for Carl and Barbara to wear for your final scenes."

Zane stepped forward and looked intently at both the models' faces. "Oh, my, God! They're flawless! Even their eyes!" He looked at Harri. "You're a godsend, Harri! Thank you!"

"It's my pleasure. Oh, I even programmed vocoders with their voiceprints so any sounds either make will actually sound like Beth and Bri. You can finish the shoot with your stars. Just do one thing?"

"Name it! A raise? Bonus?"

"Nah, nothing for me… just dedicate the episode to Bethany…"

▼▼

Elise signed for the package delivered to their apartment on Christmas Eve and closed the door. "Harri, you got a special delivery."

Harri accepted it from Elise and looked at the sender's label. "It's from the studio."

"Were you expecting something?"

"No, I don't even report for another shoot until the middle of January." She tore open the outer wrapping and cut open the box tape with a knife from the kitchen. Inside was a well-cushioned DVD with a note that simply read "Play Me".

Harri turned down the living room lights, except for the Christmas tree and other decorations, put it in their DVD player, and the ladies sat on the couch as the TV automatically came to life.

The first thing that appeared on the screen was:

In Memory of Bethany Heyward

Then the screen faded to black, followed with...

Dedicated to Harri Lewis for finishing Bethany's story

"Aw, that's so sweet!" Elise said as she put an arm around Harri's neck and kissed her cheek. She looked back at the TV as the Halloween episode for the next year began to play… when movement outside the window caught her attention. "Harri! Look!" Elise leapt from the couch and ran to the window with Harri following behind her.

They both watched as a light snow fell outside. "Well, son of a gun," said Harri. "It never snows here!"

Elise lifted the window and slid the screen open so she could stick her head out. "It's beautiful!" She turned her head to look up and gasped. "Harri! Look! Up!"

Harri went to another window and opened it to look out and up. Straight above their apartment building a single star sparkled through the light flurry.

"There's only one star!" Elise exclaimed. "Just one star in the sky!"

Harri smiled. "Merry Christmas, Bethany." She turned to her roommate. "Merry Christmas, Elise…"

RUSHMORE TO JUDGEMENT

CHAPTER 1

"I would prefer NOT to go to my Christmas party with bullets in me, and shit in my 'do!" Agent Seeker of the Task Force field team looked around and fired his .45 automatic into the dark night at the source of incoming bullets. "Just why the hell did anyone want to attack the Korean War Veterans Memorial during the Christmas season, anyway?" He ducked his head, narrowly dodging the bullet that bounced off the corner of the Lincoln Retail and Refreshments building. His standard-issue black uniform was already peppered with concrete dust.

Beside him was the field team leader, Agent Spy, dressed similarly, except Seeker wore black computerized cocoon glasses. He had a full black hood with black lenses over his head. "Tell me about it. My company's Christmas party is in thirteen hours in Richmond." said Spy calmly. He peered around and fired three shots from his own .45 automatic. "Just try very hard not to hit any of the soldier statues, ok?"

"Damn straight, man," replied the other agent. "My grandpa served with a coupla them back in Germany."

Spy tapped the side of his hood, opening a signal to their home office command center only a few miles away. "Tactical, Spy."

"Spy, Tactical 3," said a female voice on the other end of the transmission.

"Any read on the targets?"

"No, Spy. They read cold on the satellite."

Seeker added, "Could they be wearing heat-masking gear?"

"Would make sense," said Spy. "So, guess we'll have to do it the hard way."

"You're not gonna do that—" he turned around to face his leader and saw no one "—disappearing act of yours." Seeker put his gun in his holster and waited. Seeker watched the computer display on the inside of his glasses as he heard intermittent gunshots nearby, but he didn't react until he saw an icon blinking on and off in his left lens. He drew his weapon and pointed it down Daniel French Drive Southwest toward Independence Boulevard. A figure ran past him. "I suggest you stop before I blow your damn head off, asshole!" he shouted out. Seeker pointed his weapon at the fleeing figure who turned toward him in surprise, a green laser light stopping dead center of his chest. The man stopped, stared at the tiny green dot that illuminated his uniform over his heart, and raised his hands.

He stepped toward the standing figure, who was wearing a black uniform similar to his own, but not so-well fitted. There was a tear across the back of the fabric, explaining why he suddenly saw his quarry in his lens sensor. "Please move, give me a reason," Seeker chided as he reached forward to take the P23L .38 pistol from the man's right hand. Seeker gave an envious whistle when he saw the weapon. "Nice piece. Fifteen round mags, too. Not bad for a scumbag." He tucked it in the back of his own gun belt and began to pat him down in search of other weapons, but found none. "Okay, kneel down, put your hands in your pockets and make fists, then sit your ass all the way down."

His captive silently complied. Seeker stepped around in front to view his prisoner's face. "What a surprise. Standard mid-eastern male. Tactical 3, tie in and ID."

"Copy," said Tactical 3.

"Fool," said the man. "You should be with us, African. You come from Islamic lands."

"I come from College Park," Seeker chided. "Don't let my beautiful light chocolate skin deceive you. I ain't no 'African-American' or other hyphenated label. I'm an American, period. And I beat your scrawny ass."

"You beat no one," the man said.

Seeker heard in his ear, "Seeker, Tactical 3. You have Aaben Ashaz, wanted for murder and terrorism in several North and South American cities."

Seeker placed the muzzle of his weapon on Ashaz' forehead. "Well, well, Aaben. You've been a busy boy. I hope you don't have any other plans for Christmas."

Aaben spat at Seeker's feet. "Christmas, bah. There is no other god to worship but Allah. You will be killed, like the infidel you are."

"You know," said Seeker, "I'm really tired of the same terror talking points you fools spout."

"I don't care," said Aaben. "Deep down you are terrified of the coming jihad against all westerners."

Seeker looked past Aaben's head and smiled.

"What's so funny, black man?"

"I think you're about to experience real terror." Seeker holstered his gun, lifted Aaben to his feet by the upper arms and spun him around before Aaben could remove his hands from his pockets. Aaben faced the heavily-muscled black figure of Spy, standing only a couple feet from him. Spy reached one black leather-gloved hand forward, grasped Aaben by the shirt front, and lifted him a foot in the air. Seeker leaned forward and whispered to Aaben, "You might want to do exactly what he says."

Spy turned around with Aaben still elevated in his grasp and walked back into the shadows. Seeker leaned against the monument thinking, *I hope he never finds out that sometimes he scares ME..."*

CHAPTER 2

In the parking lot of the secret Task Force Division headquarters outside Washington, D.C., Spy and Seeker, in their civilian identities of Mark Jason and Calvin Geffers, walked to their respective cars. "So," said the bearded Mark, president of Jason Enterprises in Richmond, "what does a rich secret agent like you do for Christmas?"

Calvin leaned against his silver Porsche. "Well, I'm trying to decide if I wanna call Steph."

"Steph? As in Stephanie Anderson?" asked Mark. "I hear tell you two aren't on the best of terms."

"Well," Calvin admitted, "presently, she is kinda pissed off at me, but I figure 'nuff time's gone by that I can try again with her."

Mark walked to his side. "Try 'what' with her, exactly?"

"Man, you know!"

Mark smiled. "I know what, exactly?"

"You know—spoil her like she likes, dinner out,

maybe some heavy romance after."

This time Mark laughed. "You're something. Look, Cal, if you really want to win this lady over, you gotta plan for more than dinner and getting her into bed. You're not James Bond, getting the lady after every mission You're former military, act like it."

"That's brutal, man."

"And lose the long Goldilocks. Get your military cut back."

"We talkin' 'bout my love life, or yours?"

"I got a daughter joining the Navy."

Calvin nodded. "Got me there."

Mark placed a hand on Calvin's shoulder. "If you really like this lady, start treating her like a walking jewel, not a conquest target."

That made Calvin laugh. "You been reading up on our, ah, 'exploits', haven't you? Yeah, everyone calls us 'fire and water'. We're really good together, especially on joint department missions, but when we're pissed at each other...well, hell ain't got nothin' on her when she's on fire mad." He looked at Mark. "Guess that's why I like her...so unpredictable."

"Where does she live?" Mark interjected.

"Charleston," Calvin replied.

"West Virginia?"

"South Carolina."

Mark put a hand on Calvin's shoulder. "Plan a vacation, my friend. Go to her hometown, spend some downtime on her turf. Give her the opportunity to be in charge."

Calvin laughed again. "Not a bad idea, actually. I'll do it. But," he chided, "the hair-do stays!"

Mark smiled, then turned serious. "What about Mae-

Lei? I haven't seen her lately. How's she doing?" It was the second Christmas without her fiancé, Marshall Gray, the deceased prior Task Force team leader.

"Sad or depressed, or both. As far as I last knew she was locked up in her office, or maybe she's at her apartment."

Mark said, "Why don't you go check on her? You two've known each other longer than I've known her."

"Hm, good idea."

Mark got in his car and said, as he backed up, "Go in and talk to her. Merry Christmas!"

Calvin locked his car with his key fob and walked toward the building.

Mae-Lei Komala, Agent Hunter for Task Force Division, was indeed difficult to locate. He eventually found her in the target range in the basement, where she was firing at a human silhouette paper target. The bull's eye area was peppered with bullet holes. "Doin' good, girl," he said as she stopped to reload her .357.

The tall Hawaiian looked toward him, unsurprised at his arrival. "Hey, Cal. Don't you have better plans for Christmas than hanging out at the firing range? Or is Stephanie still pissed at you this week?"

He thought for several moments. "Yeah, she's pissed, I think. Everybody's on me about making it up to her, I just don't remember what I did."

"This time?"

"Fbbbt—yeah, this time. SO," he said to change the subject, "why aren't you home with the family?"

"They decided to go on a Mediterranean cruise as their Christmas gift to each other, so the only one home is the caretaker. I got nothing else to do, so I figured I'd work on my marksmanship."

"That's bullshit, girl," he said, sitting down on a chair behind her shooting cubicle. "You're avoiding it."

"I'm avoiding nothing."

"This is your second Christmas with Marshall gone. You two were supposed to be married by now. Maybe even have your first little special agent to spoil on Christmas morning."

"Keep that up and I may shoot you," she teased harshly. She took a deep breath and apologized. "I'm sorry, Cal—I just—It's—I don't feel it. I don't feel anything. I just want to shoot."

"Yeah, I got that." He slapped his hands on his knees and rose to walk to her side. He took the gun from her hand and took her free hand in his other. "You're not shooting Christmas this year." He started leading her toward the door.

"Where are you taking me?" she demanded.

"Away from here."

CHAPTER 3

Calvin drove his Porsche into a private area of Dulles International Airport in northern Virginia where his private 747, *The Adventure*, was parked. He called ahead to his pilot, Leroy, to enter a particular flight plan and prepare for departure.

He guided his car up into the belly of the giant aircraft to park behind a black sports car, which was his Task Force vehicle. As the automated chocks moved into place to secure the Porsche, Calvin said aloud, "Locking in place, take us up when we get clearance."

"Roger that," said Leroy's voice through speakers in the car.

From the right seat, Mae-Lei said, "Anyone else would call this a kidnapping, you know."

"But a kidnapping for a luxurious flight on one of the most modern 747s on Earth?" Calvin asked in reply.

She smiled. "Yeah, it's a top-flight kidnapping, pun absolutely intended."

One of Calvin's staff helped her out of the car and

escorted her up the circular stairs to the residential level of the aircraft. "Please buckle up as we prepare for takeoff," he said.

Calvin followed right behind. "Thank you, Jeremy. Once we're in the air would you mind bringing us a couple Glenfiddich's please?"

"Of course, sir."

As they waited for takeoff, Mae-Lei pointed aft toward a closed door. "What's back there?"

"My bedroom. I'll give you the grand tour once we're in flight." He tapped a button on the table between their seats. "At your discretion, Lee."

"Copy," came Leroy's voice over the table speaker. "Just got confirmation to taxi, we'll be wheels-up in just a few minutes."

As the giant aircraft began to roll forward, Mae-Lei asked, "Just how does a government secret agent afford a plane like this, even with our very generous salaries?"

"Friends in international places. Nothing in our charter says I can't make extra income."

"I know, but really!"

"And playing the stock market very well."

"Very well indeed."

Leroy's voice came over the cabin speaker. "Stand by for take-off." Moments later they felt the increased G-force as the plane advanced forward, and angled upward, soaring into the afternoon skies…

⊙⊙⊙

"You're allowed to change the color, not that I don't like black," Calvin said as he nodded toward Mae-Lei's exposed toenails in her open-toe boots.

"'Ele'ele," she corrected.

"A Hawaiian color?"

She chuckled. "Nah. That's Hawaiian for 'black'."

He laughed.

"So, old man, what are we doing cruising at thirty-thousand feet?"

"Just having a couple drinks, two old friends."

Her Hunter instinct kicked in. "Yeah, cruising around at $25,000 per hour makes for a couple very expensive drinks." She took a sip of her drink. "It's a beautiful jet for your home, though. Don't blame you for not buying a brick house somewhere."

"Who says I don't have one? Or two?"

"You've done well for yourself, I'm glad."

He took a sip from his own glass. "So have you. Buying a home next to your parents' in Hawaii, paying for their own repairs and updates. Yet you still live in that apartment you were given when you were originally recruited into Task Force. So, I'm a little extravagant and you're thrifty, we're each unique. Hell, our new leader has an international company and our fourth member does Hollywood monster movies with a couple Oscars on her shelf. We're all paid well for putting our lives on the line each mission."

She nodded in agreement. "You're right." After another sip and long pause, she went back to the prior topic. "It's just—I figured one or the other of us would find the other passed away sometime in the future. Not dead behind a building with a bullet through the head before we ever said 'I do'."

He took her hand. "We all grieved with you."

Mae-Lei put her other hand on his. "And it was appreciated." Calvin noted she didn't cry. "There's just no—

no—"

"Finality?"

"Yeah. Even though Mark was very creative in giving Marshall's killer a final damning lesson before killing him in that gunfight, there's just really no closure." She changed her tone, saying, "So, what is this trip really about, old man?"

He put his drink down and took a deep breath. "I'm keeping a promise. One Marshall and I made to each other as the last two original Task Force members…"

CHAPTER 3
A FEW CHRISTMASTIMES AGO

Agents Marshall "The Spy" Gray, and Calvin "The Seeker" Geffers were taking gunfire from above. They hid in a grassy canyon behind the Mount Rushmore mountain, returning fire carefully so as not to hit the granite top and accidentally create a crevice that could eventually expand and damage one of the sculpted presidents' heads. Both were dressed in matching black uniforms and large black cocoon glasses. The interiors of the lenses were miniature digital readout screens from their tactical aids located in Washington, D.C., monitoring their activity via dedicated overhead satellites.

"Man," complained Seeker, "every time I go on a mission with you, I get shit in my 'do'." He ducked his head as a bullet bounced off a protective boulder."

"You and your damn 'do," said Spy as he bent around his side of the boulder and fired upward. "Wish I could order you to cut that damn hair back to a military standard."

"I may, whenever I see you start covering some of

your gray," the caramel tone-skinned agent replied.

Spy pointed his .45 automatic past Seeker. "One of us has to get to that stairway and get up to the maintenance building behind Washington's head."

"Uh, huh, you actually sayin' you want me to go up that stairway and get my head shot off."

"With all that hair? Your head will be perfectly protected."

"I just wanna know why Spy was sent on a basic 'catch-the-terrorist' mission. Ain't no secret stuff here. I should be gettin' my ass shot off with Hunter."

"You know—" Spy fired upwards once more after a bullet just missed his head. "—she and Proteus are working on that hijacking over Omaha."

"Yeah, I know." Seeker fired at the top of the mountain. "Fine, you cover me, but if I get shot I'm gonna kick your ass."

"You should be fine. Upgraded uniforms from Jason Enterprises have a new Kevlar layer inside the fabric."

"Yeah, I'll believe it when I don't bleed."

Spy fired three more times into the sky and ejected the spent magazine, replacing it with a spare from his weapon belt and fired again. Seeker bolted for the steps behind Washington's side of the mountain. They remained in touch with each other via the ear communication units they wore.

Two thirds of the way up Seeker heard Spy say calmly, "Wanna haul your ass a little more, Commander? I have two magazines left."

"Bitch, bitch, bitch," Seeker replied. "You try running up these stairs without getting caught by a bullet."

"Tactical two to Seeker," the agent heard in his comm. "The third terrorist has moved inside the work shed."

"Well, shit," Seeker grumbled as he continued advancing. "Sounds like an ambush waiting. I'm open to suggestions, Spy."

"Did you pack a compression gun?" Spy asked.

"By chance, yeah."

"And a smoke timer?"

"I got what you have in mind. I'm close enough that it might work." Seeker holstered his .357 and withdrew a derringer-size pistol from a pouch on his weapon belt at the small of his back. From another pouch on the right side he removed a smoke bomb pellet, and from a third a small air-bullet with a barrel stem. He assembled the pieces and aimed toward the maintenance shed above. "Hope there's not much wind up there," he whispered as he fired the small gun.

On the back of George Washington's head, two men stood with AK-47 rifles while the third was inside the shed. The two men outside, brothers Terry and Michael Harper, were there to plant explosives to destroy the presidential monument as a protest against "government intrusion and oppression". Their companion, Diego Sanchez, was an arms-specialist militant. "How much longer?" Michael asked.

"Just hold your ass," Diego grumbled back. "We want this thing to blow correctly but not with us still here. Gotta finish assembling the wires."

"Well, hurry, man," said Terry. "We're starting to run low on ammo against those guys down there."

"Who are those guys?" Michael asked as he fired down at the two men in black.

"Cops of some kind, no doubt."

Terry ducked his head as a bullet zoomed by. "I really don't give a damn. But right now, they've got our only way down blocked!"

A cloud of smoke suddenly appeared around the

shed. "Oh, crap," Michael said. "They're tryin' to smoke us out!"

"Sounds like you've got a big problem then," Diego yelled. "This thing is primed and ready, so you better get us a clear path offa this thing, or we're going with it!"

Spy and Seeker heard in their comm units, "Satellite detectors have picked up a signal from the mountain top."

"Son of a bitch, they've armed their bomb!" Spy said angrily. "Seeker, we gotta move now!"

"Shit, I'm gonna hate all this in the morning," Seeker growled as he ran up two steps at a time. "Spy, you better be haulin' your ass, too!"

"I won't reach it in time, Cal," Spy answered. "This one's all yours, man. Get it done!"

Seeker neared the top of the steps to a walking platform near the shed. As he neared the edge of the smoke, he started firing randomly just to scare back the terrorists. He heard a scream as a bullet made contact. He reached a body on the ground as he entered the smoke; it was a man, dead from a bullet through the heart. Knowing there were two more men, he didn't hover over the body more than a couple seconds before resuming the hunt in the smoke.

Unfortunately, he wasn't fast enough; Terry saw him through the smoke first and fired, hitting the Task Force agent in the upper leg, sending Seeker to the ground beside Michael's body. Just as Terry was about to make the kill shot, his head kicked back and he, too, fell dead on the top of Washington's head.

Seeker looked over to see Spy's arrival and move through the smoke toward the shed.

Spy's black cocoon lenses were in infrared mode so he could look for the third terrorist as he came out of the shed.

A few seconds later, Diego never saw the man who killed him.

In the shed, Spy looked at the activated bomb. "Tactical, Spy. I'm looking at a non-nuclear explosive on a 75-second countdown. I'm open to suggestions."

Knowing that his tactical opposite could see what he saw via the camera in his glasses, he waited until he heard, "How's your throwing arm?"

"Not funny," said Spy as he gripped the plastic-explosive bomb and timer. "Too heavy to throw, not enough time to get it off Rushmore." To Seeker he called, "You have any helium on you?"

Seeker limped into the shed, blood running down his right leg. "Just a couple compression bombs."

"I'll take 'em." Spy took Seeker's quarter-size bombs and removed his gun belt, detaching the flat steel buckle with the diamond-engraving on the surface. He removed the standard-issue compression bombs from his own gun belt and took everything to the rear of the shed near the platform behind Washington's head. He stripped off the equipment pouches from the leather belt and folded it between the metal buckle plate and the foot-square bomb. "When I'm clear, you shoot below the plate!" he ordered Seeker as he ran away from the bomb.

Seeker fired his gun, hitting the compression bombs on the first try. The concussive blast forced the metal buckle upward, with the leather belt as insulation against the larger bomb, into the air...to safely explode several yards away from the batholiths in the sky above Peter Norbeck Scenic Highway.

The agents sat in the clearing air, surrounded by the three dead bodies. "You know, there's better ways to make a statement than to blow up another man's work," Spy said, breathing heavily.

"No kidding," Seeker agreed. "You better send these suits back to production, didn't stop this bullet from getting through."

Spy looked at Seeker's wound. "Yeah. I'll give our Jason Enterprises contact a call when we get back."

Seeker took off his black glasses and leaned back on his palms. "Hey, Gray, do me a favor?"

"Anything, pal, you know that."

"Promise me that if anything happens to me in the future, you tell Stephanie for me."

Spy took off his glasses as well and chuckled. "Wish...um...there was a way you could do that for me, too."

Calvin punched Marshall's arm. "You ass. You think no one knows you and Mae-Lei aren't banging each other? Ever since that 'undercover' mission you two have been very under-the-covers together!"

"Um, ears?" Marshall said, pointing at the comm units in the ears.

"We heard nothing," said Marshall's tactical support in Washington before the line disconnected.

"Oops," Calvin said. "Anyway, I just had an idea, since we both kinda-sorta have a someone-special."

"I'm listening."

"Let's go make a special video to our girls, and only show them some time after we're gone...maybe at Christmas."

"Christmas after. The first one will be hard enough as it is...or will be, something like that."

Calvin nodded his head. "And I got an even greater idea how to do it the best way ever..."

CHAPTER 5
NOW

"I got this idea from a Star Trek episode," Calvin told Mae-Lei. "This holographic tech is still in development, but it's getting better. For the best experience, we did this in virtual reality." He guided her to a chair in the Louisville Science Museum and placed a state-of-the-art VR headset on her. He plugged it into his iPhone and brought up a special password-protected video file.

"This better not be one of your porno videos with Stephanie," she teased.

"Not as good, no—just watch." He pressed "play".

Mae-Lei watched the view before her eyes. It turned into a view of Sandy Beach on Oahu, just in sight of Diamond Head. It was a perfect morning, clear blue skies, and no one else on the beach just yet. A familiar figure stepped into view: Marshall Gray, her deceased fiancé.

"Hi, Mae," he began, "if you're watching this it means you're nearing the second Christmas since my passing.

"Not exactly the kind of Christmas present I ever

wanted you to get from me, but that's the promise Cal and I made to each other on top of Mount Rushmore. Anyway—I never thought I'd fall in love with someone, since the military then Task Force had my full attention. Sure, there were the dalliances and regular girlfriends...there was just something about you that I had no defense against. I fell so much in love with you…" Marshall ran his hand through his graying hair. "Remember here? The first place we went after...that mission. Had lots of Lava Flows. I think that was the first time anyone ever drank me under the table first...well, into the sand.

"I want to apologize for not being there with you," he continued, "but we knew what kind of business we were in when we got close...hell, when we fell in love. I hope, though, that the time we had together was the best either of us ever had.

"You gave me the best present in the world, Mae. You have me your heart when I never asked for it, just as I gave you mine when you didn't ask for it. It was just the right thing for both of us." He chuckled. "You were the one who made my life perfect. I hope I did the same for you. But, it's okay to stop grieving, if you still are. Don't say you will never love again...you will. It'll be different, but it will be love and it will be okay. I want you to be happy. Be happy for me. That's my last Christmas present request. Go make another guy as happy as you made me. My dearest Pilialo, that would make me the happiest man on earth...well, anywhere. Merry Christmas, ku'u aloha. Until we meet again…"

The VR feed ended.

Mae-Lei slowly removed the headset and held it in her lap. Calvin stepped to her side and gently reached for her hand. "You okay, Mae?"

She grasped his hand in hers and looked up at him, eyes crying but mouth smiling. "Thank you."

He smiled back at her. "Merry Christmas, Mae."

"Merry Christmas, old man." She squeezed his hand as he stepped away to give her a few moments to herself. "Merry Christmas, Marshall...I love you...I'll see you again, my Pilialo...just be patient?"

She rose and set the VR headset on the seat. As she joined Calvin she asked, "You ever have a Lava Flow?"

CHAPTER 6
CHRISTMAS EVE

The crew members with families left to celebrate Christmas with their spouses and children. The skeleton crew staffing *The Adventure* had nowhere else to be so they decorated the living room area forward of Calvin's bedroom with a tree and lights. Presents were piled under the tree, and everyone worked together to make a delicious turkey dinner with the trimmings.

Calvin was in the middle of the activity, making his grandma's special baked beans. Her recipe went with her when she passed, so he went with sensory memory and when it smelled right, he declared it ready. Between stirs and gentle spice additions he checked his phone constantly. "Waiting for a call?" asked Carol, the southern brunette who was the head chef on *The Adventure*.

He smiled politely. "Well, was kinda-sorta," he replied.

She returned his smile. "I'm holding out for you, Mister C. It's not Christmas just yet."

"You're right as always, Carol."

She sniffed his pot of beans. "Mmm, smells like your best pot yet!" Carol got the potatoes au gratin from the oven when the timer went off and took it to the adjacent dining room. Calvin continued slowly stirring.

The hail tone went off in the plane's speaker system. Calvin reached up to press the reply button. "Go," he said.

"There's someone at the forward hatch asking to board," replied the voice of the on-board security guard.

"On my way," he replied. "Carol, mind coming back to stir for another five?"

Carol returned to the kitchen and took the spoon handle from him so he could tend to his summons.

When he reached the forward hatch below the flight deck, the tall black man in a gray suit and Christmas tree pin on one lapel acknowledged his arrival. "Who we got?" Calvin asked as he approached.

A platinum-blond-haired woman leaned in the open door. "Hi, big boy," said Stephanie Anderson.

He was surprised. "Steph? What the hell are you doing here?"

She looked aghast. "What? That's the way you say hello when I come all this way—" He stopped her with a strong warm hug, feeling her relax in his grasp. "Okay, that's better—oh yeah, much, much better."

He pulled back, asking, "Not that I'm not grateful, but I didn't expect to see you. Figured you'd just call. And when did you go Marilyn Monroe on me?"

She fingered her hair. "Thought I'd give you a little Christmas surprise. I was here in D.C. for a meeting, thought I'd stop by on my way home. So, you like the new look?"

"Oh, yeah," he said. "Thank you, Brian." The guard nodded with a smile while Calvin escorted his on-again/off-again girlfriend. "So, where are we tonight? Making up or having a nice dinner with the staff?"

"Honestly," she answered, "I've been so busy I forgot why I was mad at you, so it's a nice dinner with the staff." She'd been on his home-with-wings many times and knew many of his crew lived on the plane with him.

"I made gramma's beans…"

"You know how to turn a girl on…"

CHAPTER 7

Calvin and Stephanie relaxed in their hotel room on Folly Beach, just south of Charleston, South Carolina. They were still in bed after a wonderfully romantic night, and she had gotten up just long enough to make them each a cup of coffee before getting back under the sheets with him. "Wow," she said. "Don't think we've gone a whole three months without an argument before." She rolled off his chest to kiss his cheek. "I love you."

He kissed her in return. "I love you back."

His cell phone rang first, with hers joining in seconds later. Instinct told both of them to answer their summons. "Seeker," he said. "Agent Anderson," she said. They answered their calls and hung up.

"Rain check on another day in bed?" Calvin said as he got up and went to his suitcase, removing his black Task Force uniform.

"Hope to be back here in a couple hours myself," she said as she started putting on her blouse, forgetting her bra in the urgency. As she tugged up her panties and reached for her black slacks, Kevlar vest, blouse and jacket, she asked, "How long does it normally take you to solve a kidnapping, anyway?"

He zipped up his uniform front and waved his hand over the closure to bio-magnetically seal it. "Always too long…"

CONTINUED IN "TRAIL OF THE TALON"

97

THE AUTHORS
AND FOUNDERS OF YBR PUBLISHING

JACK GANNON

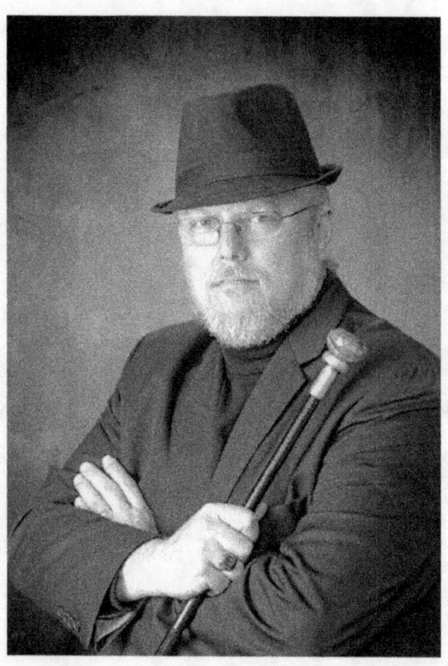

Jack Gannon began his literary career with high school best friend Cyndi Williams-Barnier after they were both retired from their respective careers, writing the stories they talked about way back in high school. Together they have written nine books, both self-published and by a publisher.

YBR Publishing was born when Jack wrote and published his first solo book, "I WALKED IN SANTA'S BOOTS", a coffee table-sized autobiography about his quarter-century as Santa Claus for Beaufort, SC. "SANTA" was entered into the Beaufort County Library Historic District Collection as an important book reflecting the history of Beaufort, SC.

His decades in print media gave him the experience to put together that first book in a unique and attractive scrap-book style, and now serves as the Production Manager for YBR Publishing. Jack works one-on-one with each author to create a distinctive visual signature in the book from cover to cover, a trademark style individual to each author with YBR Publishing. In addition, Jack is YBR Publishing's webmaster.

Jack also serves on the Liturgy Committee for St. Peter's Catholic Church in Beaufort as its chairman and the Proclaimer Ministry chair, plus scheduling all the laity for the regular weekend and special Masses.

He is retired from The Beaufort Gazette & The Island Packet after 24 years in management plus another ten years prior as a motor route delivery carrier and intern reporter.

Jack lives in Beaufort, SC, with his wife Mendy; Tasia, a 13-year-old Pomeranian; and Mister Earl Grey, a 5-year-old Russian Blue who is "a lot of cat"!

CYNDI WILLIAMS-BARNIER

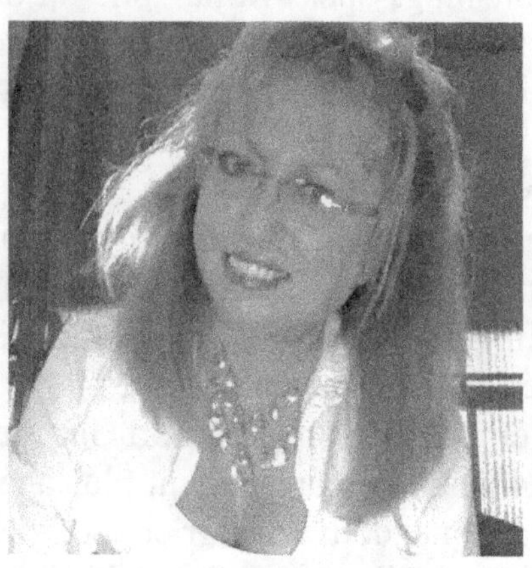

Cyndi Williams-Barnier, a Beaufort, South Carolina native, brings to YBR 25 years of county government service in Emergency Management, including writing and managing grants, writing training programs and detailed multi-agency operations manuals for disaster preparation and recovery. Her detailed programs are still used as guideposts for county, state and federal agencies including FEMA, Homeland Security and the National Guard at the Pentagon.

As co-founder of YBR Publishing and co-author of nine books, she brings a unique personal perspective and experience to maximize marketing opportunities for YBR and its authors. Her eye for detail and creative skill bring the emotional connection to every manuscript.

Cyndi lives in Ridgeland, SC, is married to Bill Barnier, and has three adorable cats (who serve as her personal YBR critics)!